THE "OH SHIT" FACTOR

Waste Management
for Our Minds

Jerry Jampolsky, M.D.

Publisher
Mini Course Publishing
www.minicourseforlife.com
3001 Bridgeway Suite K-368
Sausalito, CA. 94965 U.S.A.
info@ohshitfactor.com

Illustrator Dave Thorne
Editor Gayle Prather
Book design Julie Ruffo

Library of Congress
Cataloging-in-Publication Data
Jampolsky, Gerald G.
1. Waste Management 2. Shit
3. Forgiveness 4. Attitudinal Healing
5. Change 6. Love
ISBN 978-0-9798315-1-5

DEDICATION

This book is dedicated
to all those who at one time or
another
during their lives
have felt that they were
drowning in shit
and thereby were reminded
that they were human.
Know with great certainty
that this book was meant for you.

ACKNOWLEDGEMENTS

I wish to acknowledge my wife, Dr. Diane Cirincione, for her infinite patience, constant loving support, and her wise suggestions which were catalysts for allowing this book to come to completion.

I would like to thank Dave Thorn for his insightful cartoons which added so much to this book.

I would also like to thank Gayle Prather for her editing prowess.

Table of Contents

MY QUALIFICATIONS

Understandably, you may be wondering what my qualifications are for writing a book about shit. Although limited, I do believe that I have some expertise in this area that I would like to share with you. My experience began toward the end of World War II in 1945, when I was a 20-year-old Apprentice Seaman stationed at San Leandro Naval Hospital near Oakland, California. The hospital was used primarily as a receiving center for psychiatrically ill casualties who had served in Asia.

My primary duty as a medical corpsman was to give enemas to the patients and clean the toilets daily (which was especially important on Saturdays for the Commander's inspection). The Commander used a white glove, and if everything wasn't absolutely spotless, I would not get my weekend leave. (I failed to get my weekend leave more times than I care to remember!)

One day, a civilian friend of mine asked how I was enjoying being in the service. I told him that I thought my duty was awful, as was the food. I complained, as most of us did, that we had S.O.S. three times a week for breakfast. When he asked what that was, I explained it was soggy toast with heavy gravy that my fellow seamen and I referred to as "shit on a shingle."

I added that between giving enemas and cleaning toilets, I also thought I had the shittiest job in the hospital. How I regret saying those words! I eventually learned the hard way that my thoughts and words create my reality.

A couple of months later, I was transferred to the hospital laboratory. I became the assistant to the person in charge of examining the feces of everyone who entered the hospital. Many of the patients' stools had parasites that the men had picked up on their overseas tours. My hands and nose were literally in shit all day long.

About four months later, the guy who was in charge of the Feces Examining Department was transferred to another hospital. I then became the new department head. From then on, I was no longer addressed as "Apprentice Seaman Jampolsky," but instead was called the "Head Shit Man."

My self-esteem suffered quite a bit from that title. In a desperate attempt to raise my feelings of self-worth, I decided to give myself another designation. So I made up something with a more a scientific ring to it. I began referring to myself as a "shitologist." I much preferred that!

So now that you know all about my experience in shitology, I hope you will agree that my personal background gives me a certain authoritative gravitas for writing a book with the four letter S-word in its title.

INTRODUCTION

Before going any further, I want to say that it is not my intention to offend anyone with the language in this book. If the word "shit" happens to bother you, I apologize and trust that you will know what word you usually employ as a substitute. However, I would like to point out that the *Urban Dictionary* states that "shit" may be one of the most powerful, functional, and versatile words in the English language. To an extremely large part of the population, male and female, young and old, the word "shit" has a deep, visceral meaning.

Believe it or not, "The Oh Shit Factor" is about inner healing and spiritual awakening. It's about taking control of our thoughts and actions so that we can learn to live more peaceful, happy, and loving lives.

In this book, "shit" is used as a metaphor for the fearful, negative, angry, hateful, revengeful, and unforgiving thoughts we hold in our minds. It's also used as a synonym for the attack thoughts, judgments, grievances, selfishness, greed, self-condemnation, and guilt that we alone put into our minds, thereby creating our own personal sewers.

Writing this book has been on my mind and gurgling around in my gut for about five years now. Some people advised me not to write it because it might harm my reputation. But I am

84 years of age, and I believe I can let go of any ego needs for approval and do what my intuitive gut directs me to do in terms of being helpful.

I like to think of the benefits rather than the deficits of aging. When I was invited to say a few words at a friend's 60th birthday party, I said, "Sixty is a wonderful age because you no longer care what people say about you. But when you're 84, things get even better because you no longer remember what people said about you."

I finished this book about two years ago, but did not feel guided to have it published until now. For the last two years, I stored my manuscript in a freezer to avoid any leakages or smells that might emanate from a book about shit.

The tipping point for my decision to go ahead with publication occurred when I discovered the book *On Bullshit* (Princeton University Press, 2005), which was on *The New York Times'* bestseller's list. Written by Dr. Harry G. Frankfort, a distinguished Professor Emeritus of Philosophy at Princeton University, this short but scholarly work gives insight and understanding into a commonly used word.

Reading *On Bullshit* was like getting a message from the universe telling me that the time had come for me to publish my own "shit" book. But I want you to know right from the start that in contrast to Professor Frankfurt's scholarly treatise, my book, instead of being scholarly, is written from the gut.

Because of what is happening in the world today and with so many people feeling like they're drowning in shit, this seems to be an ideal time to bring this book out. With the financial crisis bringing financial insecurity to people across the globe, with so many people losing their homes or jobs, and so many holding on to anger and blaming those who were supposed to watch over their finances so that they could retire with a feeling of safety and comfort, it seems to me that there really are no words to adequately describe the feelings that these situations produce inside our psyches.

In my experience, when an unexpected crisis occurs in our lives, the most common response is, you guessed it: "OH SHIT!" The shock, despair, depression, blame, anger and the awful sensation in the middle of our gut are feelings that often transcend words. To heal, it is important to get in touch with these feelings and be able to communicate them. If "Oh Shit!" seems to cover these complex feelings in a way most of us can instantly relate to, then my history of shitology will serve us well.

In this book, you'll discover that the road to health is to be aware of your inner feelings, and that saying or thinking, "Oh shit!" can actually result in a greater sense of resiliency and a more balanced state of being. It's healthy to recognize when you've stepped in a pile of shit so you can say, "Oh shit," clean off your shoe and move on. The last thing you want to do is get stuck in shit.

As a society, we seem to be in the midst of a global "oh shit" moment. We can almost hear the guttural cries of "oh shit" around the world as homes are foreclosed on, jobs are lost, college tuition becomes a serious challenge, and buying food and caring for yourself and your family is a daily struggle.

Perhaps many more people than you realize are saying, "I am drowning in shit," "Someone just shit on me," "Shit happens in life, but never like this," or "I am stuck so deep in shit that I'll never be able to dig out." Be careful because these thoughts can become self-fulfilling!

If statements like these have a place in your memory bank, please keep reading because what follows has the potential to dramatically change your life by allowing you to let go of the shit in your head, with the happy side-effect of helping you to laugh more easily at yourself and at life.

PART ONE:

The Bad News
and the Good News

The bad news is that we have fallen into an ego belief system that other people's shit causes all our unhappiness, stress and lack of peace.

In fact, the world is in danger of drowning in shit as we let our ego-based voices direct us in lives filled with fear, prejudice, hatred, greed, grievances, and a lack of forgiveness, love and compassion for others as well as for ourselves. We have become afraid of love and afraid of peace.

The good news is that we can discover that it's not other people's shit causing the turmoil in the world, it's our own shit that's the culprit.

Another way of looking at it is to notice that other people's shit smells so awful that it makes us want to puke, yet the smell of our own shit doesn't seem to bother us. Dear reader, consider the possibility that if we all took responsibility for smelling our own shit and got rid of it, we could bring peace and harmony into a world that is filled with darkness and conflict.

The good news is that we can learn to transform all the shit we think people have thrown at us, all the shit we have thrown at others and all the negative thoughts we have put into our own minds. We all have the power to choose the high road by no longer putting negative thoughts into our minds, and to play an active role by transforming our negative thoughts to create a universe filled with love, light and peace. We take a giant step in our journey when we become aware that it's only our own thoughts that hurt us.

Initially I was motivated to write this book for a younger generation who might generally be uninterested in picking up a self-help book about transforming their lives. The feedback I've received since writing this little volume, however, is that this book is for many generations.

Let me be clear that I am neither condoning nor condemning the use of the word shit. I am merely exploring and highlighting its accepted use by millions of people. Shit language is very clear and not ambiguous. If someone says, "The shit has hit the fan," or "Oh shit!" no one has to go to a dictionary to figure out what the person means. The words are so visceral and graphic that we know exactly what is being communicated. For the vast majority of people, "shit" is a word of deep emotion rather than a term of vulgarity.

The Politics of Shit

The politics of shit and the politics of fear are one and the same. Where there is freedom of speech it is not uncommon, particularly during election time, to hear someone say that certain candidates or elected politicians are full of shit. Almost everyone understands clearly that this means the subjects of discussion are shading the truth, being deceptive, giving a false spin on what's true, and trying to pull the wool over our eyes.

Our egos then take hold of these perceptions to play the game of "Guilt and Blame," thereby deceiving us into believing that the cause of all our miseries is outside of ourselves. Thus do our egos find that politicians are wonderful targets for what we call "justified anger." It's helpful to look at this dynamic because so many of us assume we're being honest rather than poisoning our own minds.

A giant wake-up call for all of us is the awareness that by putting poisonous attack thoughts into our heads, we are creating a toxic environment in our minds and in our lives. We begin to recognize that perception is a mirror of our own thoughts, and not a fact. It's long past time for us to concentrate on what may be the most important waste-management challenge facing the world today: the toxic residue of the shitty thoughts that fill our heads. Our egos refuse to accept that what we see in the world is but a reflection of the thoughts and attitudes in our own minds that we are projecting outwards.

As difficult as it may be to believe, it's important to consider that we create the picture of what we see, and that our thoughts create our own reality. The image of a world that so often seems fearful and unsafe actually begins in our own minds. The law of the ego says that if something is going wrong in our lives, we should find someone else to blame. Our egos, masters of deception that they are, would have us believe that it's someone else's shit that's causing the problem, not our own.

One of the premises of this book is that we need to take responsibility for our own thoughts and feelings, and stop blaming other people. We need to become aware of our own shit and actively begin to clean out our own minds. As we do that and as we let go of the self-imposed blocks to love that we've erected, we rediscover the love that has always been in our hearts and minds.

Allowing negative thoughts to linger in our minds interferes with our health and well being, as well as with how we feel about and experience ourselves and others. Condemning thoughts (including self-condemnation) interfere with our compassion and kindness, and keep us in an unforgiving state of mind. These thoughts create wars within ourselves and with others. Often we are unaware and even in the dark about the fact that when we attack others, we are projecting something from within our own minds. Our ego minds are based on the belief that hurting others and trashing our minds, bodies and also the Earth can bring us that which we long for.

Admittedly the word "shit" is used here for shock value because the world is in such a critical state of separation, fear and unhappiness. Perhaps most of us can benefit by being shocked into the awareness that our thoughts dramatically affect every cell of our bodies and every aspect of our consciousness. Toxic thoughts are the cause of our fear and unhappiness, and they contribute to the problems we see. It is imperative that each of us becomes motivated to see the great value of getting rid of the toxic waste products (the negative thoughts) that make cesspools of our minds. It's about seeing the urgent need of owning our thoughts and attitudes by healing our split minds, and thereby healing the world we see. To be successful in cleaning up our environment, we must first clean up our own minds.

As you read on, you will discover that this book is about transforming the shit in our minds into light and love. It is about the peace, harmony and hope we experience when we see the value of cleaning out our minds and retraining them to enable us to take responsibility for what we see and what we experience.

PART TWO

The Language of Shit

It has been my observation that when we say, "Oh shit," we are using this expression as a reflexive reaction to something that happened to us very unexpectedly. Frequently, it is a response to a fearful situation. The "oh shit" response is different than the use of this four-letter word in other parts of our life.

As a child and young adult, I frequently used words like "shit" that I picked up at school. Countless times, I remember my mother spanking me and washing my mouth out with soap. In fact, as I write this, I can still taste that soap. But since I knowingly began my spiritual pathway in 1975, I no longer find myself using these words, *except* for one kind of situation—when I suddenly find myself in unpredictable or unexpectedly dangerous circumstances.

For example, if you're stopped at a traffic light, sitting there waiting for the signal to change, and from out of nowhere, a car crashes into you. Before you can even process what happened, the first two words that come out of the mouths of many people are: "Oh shit!" This happens to me with even minor situations, such as accidentally breaking a dish; again, with lightning speed I say, "Oh shit!"

It feels like a knee-jerk response that spontaneously occurs without any thoughts going through my mind. After talking to linguists and other professionals about this, I have come to the conclusion that no one seems to have an agreed-upon answer as to why so many of us seem to use "oh shit" this way. It is my impression that no one really knows why.

My tongue-in-cheek theory is that when we are suddenly in a potentially dangerous situation or we have just made what seems like a terrible or stupid mistake, the following happens: Our adrenal glands start pumping and our adrenalin rate goes through the roof. When this rush hits our bowels, out come those two words. This happens so rapidly that there's no awareness of any thoughts preceding "oh shit." It's just a reflex. It is not unknown for something to be so shocking and so fearful that people are known to say, "Oh shit," and also to simultaneously shit their pants!

My Unscientific Study

One day I became curious about this phenomenon and began a limited, completely unscientific study of how other people respond in similar situations. I talked to men and women from all walks of life. I spoke with the elderly, the young, the sophisticated, the well educated, fundamentalists, ministers, rabbis and scholars. I discovered that for the vast majority of them, the first words out of their mouths in an emergency situation were... you guessed it: "Oh shit!" Surprisingly, at least to me, an equal number of women, just like the men, responded in this way.

Recently, my wife Diane and I spent an evening with a priest, and I happened to mention the subject of the book I was writing. When we told him about the response we were getting from most people, he stood up and in a firm, authoritive voice declared, "Well, priests *never* say that!" Then, with a twinkle in his eyes, he said, "They say, "Holy shit!" We also discovered that when the black boxes that record airline cockpit conversations are examined after a fatal crash, the pilot's last words are often, "Oh shit!"

The National Transportation Safety Board recently divulged that it had covertly funded a project with U.S. automobile makers whereby similar black-box voice recorders were installed in four-wheel drive pickups and SUVs in an effort to determine the circumstances in the last 15 seconds before a fatal crash. Investigators were surprised to find that in 44 of the 50 states surveyed, the recorded last words of drivers in 61.2 percent of fatal crashes were, "Oh shit!"

In questioning people from the four corners of the earth, friends in Japan, the Netherlands, France, Italy and Argentina told us that in their countries, "Oh shit!" is very often the first thing uttered during emergencies or unexpected events. But Great Britain is different. As we have been informed, one of the most common expressions used there is, "Bloody shit!" When we took the first draft of this manuscript to be copied, the 60-something woman who waited on us laughed at the title and said, "I say that all the time, and if I don't say it, I think it."

"Shit" is bandied around quite a bit these days. It's frequently bleeped out of television shows. *The Daily Show with Jon Stewart* has shown quite a bit of expertise in using that word. And at a meeting of world leaders, upon discovering that a nearby microphone hadn't been switched off and had been picking up his private conversation with British Prime Minister Tony Blair, former President George W. Bush immediately said, "Oh shit."

I know a woman in her mid-80s who was clearly not in favor of my writing a book with a four-letter word in it. A couple of months later, she came up to me and said, "Jerry, I need to be honest with you. I say, 'Oh shit,' every once in a while when suddenly something unexpected happens to me, like breaking something or spilling a glass of water." Perhaps most of us have experienced these two words somewhere along the way, and they've become a part of our shared human experience.

The History of Shit

The history of the word "shit" is not agreed upon by authorities. The following story about manure has appeared in the literature. Some feel it is a myth, while many others believe it to be true. Either way, it makes for an interesting read.

In the 16th and 17th centuries, everything had to be transported by ship and because commercial fertilizers had yet to be invented, large shipments of manure were common. Manure was shipped dry, because in dry form it weighs much less than when wet. But once water (at sea) hit it, it not only became heavier, but the process of fermentation began again. A by-product of this fermentation is methane gas. As the stuff was stored below decks in bundles, you can see what could (and did) happen. Methane began to build up below decks and the first time someone came below at night with a lantern, *BOOM!*

Several ships were destroyed in this manner before it was determined just what was happening. After that, the bundles of manure were always stamped with the term "Ship High In Transit" on them, which meant for the sailors to stow it high enough off the lower decks so that any water that came into the hold would not touch this volatile cargo and start the production of methane.

Thus evolved the term "S.H.I.T" (Ship High In Transport), which has come down through the centuries and is in use to this very day.

A very dear friend of mine, Dan Millstein, jokes that the word "shit" must have originated on a golf course. As we go beyond the "Oh shit" reflex response, we find that men use the word to describe deep emotional feelings much more often than women do. Perhaps this is because men in general have more difficulty in expressing their deep emotional feelings. Many of us men learned this language on the playgrounds of our youth.

It is my belief that the majority of those who say, "shit" do so simply as an honest expression of the depth of their feelings around a certain situation and not as an expression of profanity. For example, when a man is telling his friend he is in the shit house with his wife, the statement may be more resonant than saying, "I am in trouble with my wife." Saying, "I was scared shitless," may be a stronger way to express emotion for many people than simply saying, "I was really frightened," or "I was very scared." Saying, "Shit happens," may have more power and force for some than saying, "Bad things are a fact of life."

Many people use "shit" in positive ways. In our culture, an individual who is a "shit disturber" is often a brave person willing to stick his or her neck out to blow the whistle about something dishonest or crooked happening in a corporation or the government. The word is used in society as a compliment, to indicate the person did something good. (Obviously, corporations or government agencies don't view these people as favorably.)

Using the language of shit in business can be humorous, lightening everyone's load. A friend sent the following email:

Good Morning Employees! Effective immediately:

In order to assure the highest level of quality work and productivity from employees, it will be our policy to keep all employees well trained through our program of Special High Intensity Training (S.H.I.T).

We are trying to give our employees as much S.H.I.T. as possible. If you feel you don't receive your share of S.H.I.T., please see your supervisor. You will be placed at the top of the S.H.I.T. list, and our supervisors are especially skilled at seeing you get all the S.H.I.T. you can handle.

Employees who don't take their S.H.I.T. will be placed in Departmental Employee Evaluation Programs (D.E.E.P. S.H.I.T.). Those who fail to take D.E.E.P. S.H.I.T. seriously will go to Employee Attitude Training (E.A.T. S.H.I.T.).

Since our supervisors took S.H.I.T. before they were promoted, they don't have to do S.H.I.T. anymore, and are all full of S.H.I.T already. If you are full of S.H.I.T., you may be interested in a job teaching others. We can add your name to our Basic Understanding List of Leaders (B.U.L.L.S.H.I.T.).

For employees who are intending to pursue a career in management and consulting, we will refer you to the department of Managerial Operational Research Education (M.O.R.E. S.H.I.T.). This course emphasizes how to manage M.O.R.E. S.H.I.T.

If you have further questions, please direct them to our Head of Teaching, Special High Intensity Training (H.O.T. S.H.I.T.).

Thank you,
Boss In General,
Special High Intensity Training
(B.I.G. S.H.I.T.)

The following story was also forwarded to me in an e-mail:

In the beginning was the Plan. And then came the Assumptions. And the Assumptions were without form. And the Plan was without substance. And darkness was upon the face of the Workers. And the Workers spoke among themselves, saying, "This is a crock of shit, and it stinks."

And the Workers went unto their Supervisors and said, "It is a pail of dung, and we can't live with the smell."

And the Supervisors went unto their Managers saying, "It is a container of excrement, and it is very strong, such that none may abide by it."

And the Managers went unto their Director, saying, "It is a vessel of fertilizer, and none may abide its strength."

And the Directors spoke among themselves, saying to one another, "It contains that which aids plant growth, and it is very strong."

And the Directors went to the Vice Presidents, saying unto them, "It promotes growth, and it is very powerful."

And the Vice Presidents went to the President, saying unto him, "This new plan will actively promote the growth and vigor of the company with very powerful effects."

And the President looked upon the Plan and saw that it was good.
And the Plan became Policy. And that, my friends, is how shit happens.

PART THREE

The Mind and the Gut

Rather than accepting that our mind is simply part of our brain, many choose instead to believe that there is one universal mind and that we are all a part of it. This universal mind is formless. If you send an angry and hateful thought out into the cosmos, it goes everywhere. The same is true for love. When we consciously send out love from our own mind, this too goes everywhere.

Imagine for a moment, if you will, that the world is made up of a giant ocean representing our universal mind. Then imagine that a small heart-shaped stone is dropped into that ocean. Imagine next that the ripple the stone creates affects every particle in the entire body of that vast stretch of water. Imagine then that perhaps this is how our minds work.

We underestimate the power of our mind and how it affects us and others, both positively and negatively. Perhaps the most important gift we have been given by the universe is the power to choose what thoughts we put into our minds. When we choose shitty thoughts, we create shit in our environment. It is important to consider that in many ways, our thoughts can be as destructive as our actions. Many of us operate as if we are on automatic pilot. Consequently, we are not tuned in to the damage that our own shitty thoughts can cause to our minds, to our bodies, and to those around us.

Isn't it time to look deeper inside our own minds and to no longer be in denial about what we are doing to ourselves? Isn't it time to go off automatic pilot, take control of the thoughts we put into our minds and free ourselves from the shackles of negative thinking? Our minds and bodies deserve to be nourished with love and not contaminated with thoughts that can keep us imprisoned in our own shit.

The Power to Choose

At this critical time, people around the world are worried about terrorism, economic instability, inflation, recession, poverty, nuclear proliferation, and global warming, as well as the question of whether we can ever learn to solve our problems without going to war. It is empowering to know that we are not helpless and that by changing what we put into our minds, we can also change our perception of reality. As we do inner healing, our outside world starts to heal as well.

If there were ever a time to choose to renounce the victim role and to change our minds about how we see ourselves and others, it is now; it is today; it is this instant. I believe it's essential that we take responsibility for retraining our minds and that we remain diligent about the thoughts and attitudes we put into them.

We can start by learning to believe that nothing is impossible. Holding on to anger, blame, and guilt is a sure way of creating a toxic condition in the mind. It creates waste products that interfere with our happiness and well being. When we choose to see the value of letting go of these thoughts, then compassion, kindness, tolerance, and gentleness flow from our hearts. Living in a consciousness of giving allows us to love others and ourselves more than we ever dreamt possible.

Blame, Guilt and Grievences

The waste products of blame result from the mistaken belief that if something goes wrong in our lives, it is someone else's fault. Please permit me to put it more succinctly and to bring it home in a way that will be hard to forget:

Wake-up call:
It is not other people's shit
that causes us to be upset!

It's our own shitty thoughts and attitudes that cause us to have a shitty life in what often looks like a shitty world. We change and clean up the world we see and experience by beginning with ourselves.

We human beings are, at times, odd ducks. We brush our teeth every day because we see value in it and are convinced that it will help us remain healthy. Most of us bathe daily for the same reason. Yet we don't seem to see the value in washing our minds daily of the waste products that our own toxic thoughts have produced and accumulated.

In order to have a life that really works and has meaning, we must find ways to get rid of the shit we put into our minds that subsequently pollutes the world. The world is drowning in and being destroyed by our collective mental garbage. By getting our own shit together, we can learn to live in harmony with others and become more consistently happy, creative, and successful in everything we do.

The Satellite Mind

For a long time, I've had a theory that we all have an invisible mind in the deep recesses of our bowels that feeds thoughts and emotions into our brains, the organ we generally associate with thoughts and feelings. This satellite mind does not have a specific form, but it *is* split into two parts. Half of it is made up of the same Unconditional Love that created us in its image. This is the mind that allows us to experience peace because it is filled with the energy of love. It is the center that connects us to our spiritual core, our intuition, our inner knowing.

Have you ever wondered where the statement, "I have a gut feeling," came from? In Western culture, it usually means one has a sense about something that bypasses the rational mind. When we're conflicted about what to do, we use this gut feeling to make a decision. No one seems to know where the idea of gut feelings originated, but everyone knows what it means and accepts its existence.

Another statement people commonly use goes a bit like this: "Something doesn't smell right about what that guy is saying." What this thought implies is that the guy is bullshitting us; not telling us the truth. So perhaps something not smelling right goes straight to our bowels to be deciphered by our satellite mind. Both of these examples point to the gut and the importance it may have for us as a center for wisdom and knowledge in making decisions. Some people call it a sixth sense.

Native Hawaiian Thoughts About the Gut

Imagine my surprise when I recently discovered that native Hawaiians have been relying on the gut for centuries.

My dear and recently deceased friend, Kanalu Young, a teacher of Hawaiian studies at the University of Hawaii, helped me understand the Hawaiian perspective on it.

In the Hawaiian language, *na'au* (pronounced nah-ow) is the word for "gut." Using Western lingo, the *na'au* would be the central powerhouse of our physical, mental, and spiritual being; the in-dwelling hub of the circle of life experience; and the home of all inner knowing. It is also the source of wisdom from which the most astute decisions are made.

A related word, *na'auao*, means inner knowing; facts and knowledge combined as one, then conveyed to others. This is the source of all positive energy and intelligence—the center for enlightenment. Think of it as the home of all interconnectedness within a human being.

In the Hawaiian culture, *na'au* is viewed as a key location with a perceivable energy or spirit. To be able to plug into the source of this energy, proper breathing (from within the stomach and gut) and chanting are essential. Learning and practicing this becomes a way of tapping into the *na'au* to develop, strengthen, and convey *na'auao*.

At times, many of us may suddenly be afraid and feel like there's a rock in our gut. But like the Hawaiians, we can learn to see this experience as a means of receiving valuable guidance.

Part of our challenge is that we are used to making decisions based only on thinking, so we're only using half of our decision-making resources. On top of that, our minds tend to become conflicted. We may recall previous decisions that didn't turn out the way we wanted. Fear comes into play because we don't want to make another mistake. Many of us assume that our lives are littered with such mistakes. And so we act from this mental state of conflict, and the results usually reflect this. We may find that we get better results, however, if we learn to respect our gut feelings, which are closely tied to our heart feelings.

The Ego Part
of Our Satellite Mind

The second half of our satellite mind is home to the ego, which is composed of fearful, negative energy. Very simply, you can look at your ego as if it were the shit maker of fear and negative thoughts that we then take into our minds. In fact, we can look at the ego in this way:

THE MAIN FUNCTION
OF OUR EGOS
IS TO MANUFACTURE
FEARFUL, ANGRY THOUGHTS
AND ATTITUDES
FOR US TO PLACE IN OUR MINDS
SO THAT WE
EXPERIENCE SEPARATION.

The primary goal of the ego is to cause conflict, pain, depression, and feelings of separation and hopelessness. Our egos want to stir up trouble, and they try to find reasons for separation because they are unable to unite with others.

The ego's enemy is peace and unconditional love because it believes only in conditional love. It comes from a place of scarcity and lack, and it's constantly looking for what it's not getting from someone else. When it doesn't get everything it wants (and it never does), the ego always blames the other person. Our egos are faultfinders, not love finders.

The simple truth is that when making either large or small decisions in life, we always have a choice to either listen to the voice of love (the voice of our heart and gut) or to the voice of fear (the ego voice).

It is always possible to see an innocent child in everyone we meet.

It is always possible to see a light in the heart of everyone we know.

It is always possible for our mind's eye to wear glasses that allow us to see only the love in others.

PART 4

The Story of Bob

This is the story of Bob, a composite of many people who suffer from the toxic thinking that I call SIMS, or Shit-In-Mind Syndrome. I'm telling this story in the hope that it will make the dynamics of SIMS clearer to the reader. Because SIMS is a term I created, you will not find it in psychiatric nomenclature, and I have no scientific data to present. I will be sharing only my own impressions and experiences working more or less as a coach and a door opener, offering choices of other ways to look at his life situation.

I am hopeful that by reading Bob's story, you will not only have a better idea how this syndrome works, but also an appreciation for the benefits that inner healing can offer for those who suffer from it.

Bob's History

Bob was 28 years old but looked much older when he first came to my office. He was married and had two children. His father was an alcoholic— very domineering and strict. His mother tended to be over-indulgent. Bob had a mid-level executive job, worked long hours, and spent much of his free time with other guys at the local pool hall. This meant that he was rarely home with his family.

Bob was often angry, opinionated, self-centered, and extremely judgmental. He tended to view others as wrong and himself as right. He ate an enormous amount of junk food, was overweight and looked unhealthy.

Bob came to see me because his wife was threatening to leave him, and despite the fact that she had made this threat before, he believed she really meant it this time.

Not being a forgiving kind of guy, Bob held on to grudges. He tended to be confrontational and abrupt with others, and he was a poor listener. He also had no insight into the fact that his unforgiving attitude toward others was related to an unforgiving attitude towards himself.

Bob had a defective sense of smell—both figuratively and literally. Despite all the garbage he put into his mind and body and the odor it caused, no deodorant could mask the smell that followed him around. He seemed disconnected from his soul.

Disharmony in What You Think, Say, and Do

I quickly made the diagnosis of SIMS. Like Bob, many people with SIMS tend to be controlling and verbally abusive. Their minds are overloaded with negative, garbage thoughts. They also tend to be deceptive and interested only in themselves. They have a "me first" kind of attitude.

Both men and women can suffer from SIMS. Like Bob, they tend to have a disharmony in what they think, say, and do. Someone with SIMS can have a smile on his or her face while at the same time thinking, "This person I'm talking to is such a jerk."

Author Hugh Prather, a good friend of mine, once shared with me something he does to help him keep garbage thoughts out of his mind. He imagines that there is a television monitor on top of his head that broadcasts all the thoughts in his mind all the time.

If you are anything like me, when you do this exercise throughout the day, you discover that you quickly become very focused on cleansing your mind of all negative or judgmental thoughts and consequently clean up your act.

Constipation of the Mind

It was also my impression that Bob suffered from constipation of the mind, a condition that, in my experience, is seen frequently with people suffering from SIMS. Those with this condition seem addicted to remembering scenes from their past and replaying them over and over again like old movies. Their minds become a combination garbage dump and cesspool that holds all their negative thoughts.

When Bob's mind became overloaded with shit, it was like his negative thoughts were inflating a balloon. The tension grew so great that the balloon eventually exploded. The results were verbal projectile diarrhea spewing everywhere, covering and infecting everyone in its path with the shitty residue from Bob's mind. Make no mistake: negative thoughts and judgments that pile up in the mind will eventually come out of the mouth.

Inner and Outer Environmental Hazards

Bob treated his environment with the same lack of respect and love that he did for himself and his loved ones. He thought nothing of tossing an empty beer can on the ground and would frequently throw refuse out his car window. He had absolutely no love for the earth and continued to treat the planet as he treated himself, like a garbage dump. In short, Bob was an environmental hazard.

Up to this point, he had ignored all the information he'd ever heard or read about why it is important to be careful about the food we put into our bodies. He also had no awareness that his thoughts and attitudes determined his actions.

Finally, Bob didn't recognize that we can't change unless we are aware of what needs changing.

Here is a cartoon of Bob at the beginning of his healing, when he first had the courage to open the door of his mind and look inside to see all the garbage he'd been keeping there.

Remember, if you decide to open the door to *your* mind, be careful, because you might be shocked at what you see and particularly what you smell!

Stepping Stones to Health

One of the first steps in Bob's road to health was his willingness to look at the shit he had put into his own mind and to begin to recognize that, just maybe, other people weren't always the ones causing his problems. That was quite a revelation for him! He began to understand that it wasn't important to try to change other people's attitudes (like his father's), but rather, it was essential for him to learn to change his own.

Bob's second step was realizing that we have the power to choose what thoughts and attitudes we put into our minds. We can choose to be miserable and pessimistic or we can choose to be happy and optimistic. Bob could also choose to make decisions based on fear and judgments or to make decisions based on love. He could choose to experience peace or conflict; he could choose to be a love finder or a fault finder; and he could choose to be a victim or not to be a victim. It was all up to him!

Bob began to see value in choosing inner peace as a goal. To help him achieve this, he also began to explore some of the painful events in his past that he was still angry about, as well as grudges he was still holding because of them. He began to understand that he had an "ego mind," and that this ego mind was the negative shit maker of his life. Bob discovered that his ego mind contained a number of rooms that he had not been consciously aware of before.

Bob's ego mind had a Room of Fear, a Game of Blame and Guilt Room, an Anger Room, a Fear Room, and a Hopelessness Room, as well as several others. He began to show a willingness to look at and to try to understand all of these rooms. Bob was quite surprised that they had no doors and did not seem to connect to each other.

In one room, Bob found that he was alone except for the voice of his father saying over and over again, "Bob, you don't deserve my love. You are never going to amount to anything.

You're stupid, and you will never be good enough."

In his own self-discovery, Bob began to see that a part of him was trying to please his dad by making him right about not being good enough. He then started to open a new door to believing in himself and to separate himself from the negative imagery that his father had projected onto him.

The Game of Blame and Guilt Room

Inside this room, Bob witnessed himself and his wife fighting with each other. The game started with Bob asking his wife to pick up his dry cleaning on her way home from work. She said that she was too busy to do it that day, so Bob immediately lobbed a guilt bomb at her. Watching himself in the "Game of Blame and Guilt" room, he recognized he had been trying to control his wife by making her feel guilty enough to do what he wanted.

Rather than doing what he wanted her to do, Bob's wife simply threw a bigger guilt bomb back at him, and the game of guilt and blame continued.

It was as if each of them stood next to garbage cans, and kept digging deeper into the cans for things they had done years ago that they could still use to wound one another. The two of them continued to throw garbage at each other until they were exhausted.

The crucial ingredient for healing any relationship problem is the willingness to no longer see value in playing the game of blame and guilt. As he began to examine how he had played the game, Bob made a crucial discovery: He realized he had superimposed his dad onto his wife, and that his *real* problems were dealing with the unhealed relationship he still had with his father.

I knew Bob was starting to make real progress when he told me, "When I throw shit or verbally attack someone, I'm going to get that shit right back in my face." That's when Bob started to believe there had to be another way of looking at himself, his wife and kids, and life in general.

Looking at the World Differently

As Bob began to open his mind to the possibility that there could be another way of looking at the world, he also started opening his mind to the reality that nothing is impossible. For those like Bob who have struggled with destructive behaviors, this truth is very freeing. Bob also found it helpful to learn that it was only his *own* thoughts and attitudes that could hurt him—the thoughts and attitudes of others (like his father's) couldn't do Bob any harm at all unless he chose to let them into his mind.

The Most Important Remedy for SIMS

Forgiveness is the answer to the challenges of waste management for our minds. It's crucial for people who are suffering from SIMS to recognize the truth of this statement.

Bob's initial reaction to our discussion about forgiveness was to tell me that he thought people who forgive everybody are weak or crazy. He believed that his wife, his boss, and many others continued to do things that were not, in his book, forgivable. Consequently, he believed that these people deserved his harsh judgments and his unforgiving, unloving attitude.

Bob also believed that holding on to anger, grievances, and revengeful feelings was a good way to protect himself. He relished proving other people wrong and himself right because this made him feel superior.

Bob decided to read two of my books, *Love is Letting Go of Fear* and *Forgiveness: The Greatest Healer of All*. As he read, he began to learn how his revengeful, unforgiving attitude was destructive to himself and others. His unforgiving attitude was actually fueling his insecurity. He gradually began to learn that anger, judgments, and unforgiving thoughts cannot be contained—they spread to everything around him. I suggested that he create a kind of mental Post-It note that said:

NEGATIVE THOUGHTS
POLLUTE EVERY PART
OF MY MIND AND HEART
AND EVERY ASPECT OF MY LIFE.

As Bob gradually changed his perception, he learned another truth: Rather than weakening us, forgiveness actually frees and empowers us to become the person that our heart wants us to become.

Just as scientists have discovered how to transform cow manure into electrical energy and light, we can use forgiveness to transform the shit we have put in our minds into light and love.

Bob and I talked about what happens

when we hold on to grievances. I showed him some articles detailing new scientific evidence that when we don't forgive, our anger actually eats us up alive, affecting the immune system as well as every organ and cell in the body. I shared my belief that forgiveness is a potent laxative for relieving the shit in our minds, and that it may in fact be the most powerful healing force in the world.

We discussed different ways of looking at forgiveness, as well. For example, I pointed out that to forgive does not mean condoning or agreeing with outlandish behavior. Likewise, forgiving someone does not necessarily mean the person you are forgiving will change his or her behavior. I reminded Bob that sometimes the first step in forgiving something that's difficult to forgive is as simple as just having the *willingness* to forgive. Finally, we talked about how forgiving others can be a stepping stone to seeing the value of forgiving ourselves.

A Sure Cure for Constipated Minds

Bob learned that forgiveness instantaneously cleanses the mind because it cleans out our inner slate of the painful, hurtful past. It is the key to happiness. Archbishop Desmond Tutu of South Africa has written many important statements, but the one he is most remembered for is this: "There can be no future without forgiveness."

Forgiveness is more potent than any medicine we can purchase at the pharmacy. Better yet, it is free. It opens the door and releases the love and peace that has always resided in our hearts.

Forgiveness, along with love, is the most important gift we can give to ourselves, as well as to others, because it awakens and ignites our spiritual core. It frees our souls to sing and dance and laugh. It allows us to walk with lighter steps.

A Visualization and Forgiveness Exercise

In the early part of our work together, Bob told me that he did not consider himself to be an abstract thinker. He asked if I had some sort of concrete exercise that he might do. Because I have dyslexia, I could easily understand his need to have something concrete. I asked if he had a good imagination, and he said that he did.

I then reminded Bob that we are told it is healthy to brush our teeth and take a bath daily. But equally as important for our health and well being is for us to wash our minds daily. I went on to explain that the exercise I had for him was like giving his mind a daily bath or shower.

I asked Bob to close his eyes and imagine that he could safely remove his brain from his skull and place it in a sink. Then, with his eyes closed, Bob put his hands on top of his head and imagined he was pulling the two sides of his skull apart and then was gently removing his brain and placing it in an imaginary sink.

Now that his brain was in the sink, I told Bob to picture black matter like hardened dirt on top of his brain, explaining that this represented the residue from the shitty thoughts and attitudes he had put into his mind. I now told him it was his job to vigorously wash away all this negative material, adding that the water he would be using was "forgiveness water" that had the ability to cleanse the hurtful memories of the past.

As Bob began to vigorously scrub his mind with the forgiveness water, I went on to explain a few other things. When we cleanse our minds of judgments, hatred, anger, guilt, blame, prejudice, and old wounds, what is left is the pure, unconditional love that has always been there. This love is like a bright light within us that surrounds every organ in our bodies. I reminded Bob of some of the attributes of unconditional love, such as joy, peace, kindness, gentleness, empathy, generosity, trust, faith, and honesty.

After ten minutes, he put his brain back in his head, stunned at the result. "I feel a lot lighter after getting rid of all that crap," he admitted.

I suggested he do the exercise with enthusiasm twice a day: upon awakening and just before going to bed. I reminded him that when we let go of the past through forgiveness, the mind no longer has those separate rooms; instead, it's unified and whole. I also explained that using forgiveness as a waste management device has to be a continuous process, like breathing or taking out the garbage. You can't do it sometimes and then forget about it when you don't feel like doing it.

At the end of the forgiveness exercise, I gave Bob a list of ten principles he might want to choose to believe. I reminded him it is only our beliefs that keep us and the world in chains. Here's the list of principles I gave Bob:

BELIEF IS A CHOICE, SO I CHOOSE TO BELIEVE THAT:

1. Nothing is impossible.

2. Everything is forgivable.

3. Holding on to grievances only hurts me and injures my health.

4. No one else has to change for me to forgive.

5. Forgiveness does not require a form.

6. By learning to forgive others, I can learn to forgive myself.

7. Forgiveness could take one second or several years, depending on what I believe.

8. My willingness to forgive is my springboard to a happy life.

9. Forgiveness is a continuous and never-ending process.

10. When I truly forgive myself or someone else 100%, I will no longer see the shadows of my past or of the past of the other person.

The New Bob

Bob soon stopped his morning habit of immediately rushing toward his "to do" list. Soon after awakening, he would instead start the morning with the following affirmation:

PEACE OF MIND
WILL BE MY ONLY GOAL TODAY.

Bob would then take 20 minutes to still his mind and do his own brand of meditation. He would say out loud: "Peace to my mind. May all my thoughts be still." He would then do his best to let all his negative thoughts disappear and then let love flow into his mind and into his heart. Bob began to discover he could have a sense of inner peace even when chaos was going on all around him.

His morning affirmation served as a rudder, keeping him on an even keel throughout the day. At night, he cleared the day from his mind and chose to have peaceful thoughts. Peace of mind became Bob's new experience.

As he worked on forgiving himself for previously insensitive and thoughtless behavior, he began to see those around him differently. Before, he acted as if the world centered on him. Now, he slowly began to experience his wife's feelings as being as important as his own and went on to believe in equality in his relationship with her and others. Bob learned the art of being a good listener, which meant listening with love and without judgment—and without interrupting the other person.

He discovered that when someone is being confrontational, there are other ways of dealing with it rather than arguing. It had never occurred to him to consider what his own role in a confrontation might have been. Much to his amazement, his relationship with his boss also began to change, as did his performance at work.

Perhaps one of the biggest gains Bob made was when he decided to take full responsibility for his own happiness. When he was able to do this, he discovered his attitude was more important than how much money he had or how big a house he lived in.

Purpose of Life

As Bob looked back over his life and the days he spent accumulating all the stuff that went into his constipated mind, he decided his new goal was to have a caring attitude and to do his best to be helpful and of service to others. That was quite a different goal from the one he had in the days when he thought his purpose was to be a self-appointed judge who decided on the guilt or innocence of others. Much to his surprise, Bob discovered that what brought him the most happiness was helping others.

Near the end of completing his work with me, Bob began to volunteer at a soup kitchen for the poor and homeless. I was amazed at how much this experience had brought out the compassion in him. He told me that he had always wondered why other people couldn't get their shit together. Now that he had more compassion in his heart, he saw other people with a clearer mind. "I now see other people as part of myself," he told me.

On his last visit, Bob came in and said he was still a work in progress. He was more energetic, his eyes were bright, and he said he had never been happier. He mentioned that his healing had not been quick nor had it been easy, and he had experienced many ups and downs during the process. But in recent days, he was feeling more peaceful and happy, and was quite excited to share with me the changes that had occurred in his life.

Bob received a promotion at work and his relationship with his wife and kids improved immensely. He felt better physically than he had in years, and he had a zest for life that had been absent for longer than he could remember. "You know," Bob said to me as he thanked me on his way out, "It would never have occurred to me in a million years that so many of the thoughts

I had been putting in my mind were poison, and that by believing those toxic thoughts, I was actually making myself unhealthy and unhappy. I held the key to happiness all along, but I never realized it! It's amazing what learning to smell your own shit can do!"

And what really fascinated me was that during that last visit, Bob smelled like a rose.

AFTERWORD

The ten guidelines for the waste management of our minds:

1. Recognize that putting shitty thoughts in your mind will give you a shitty life.

2. Remember that if you throw shit at others, it will come back and hit you in the face.

3. Understand that forgiveness will wash out all your shitty thoughts and will clean out all the waste in your mind.

4. Stay in the present and stop living in the past.

5. Take responsibility for your own happiness.

6. Decide you are not a victim, and let go of guilt and blame.

7. Decide each day not to hurt others or yourself with your thoughts or actions.

8. Remind yourself daily that love is the answer to any problem you will ever face.

9. Expand your sense of humor and learn to laugh at yourself.

10. Above all, don't get stuck in your own shit.

APPENDIX

One of my dearest friends is Jack Luckett, whom I've known for more than 30 years. During all that time, and despite the fact that Jack is a retired marine who saw combat in both Korea and Vietnam, I have never heard the word "shit" escape from his lips. When he heard I was writing this book, Jack told me that his mind had an encyclopedia of "shit words" which he kindly shared with me. I have added some additional expressions from a few other sources, as well as from the *Urban Dictionary* that can be found on the Internet.

So for those of you who wish to become more familiar with the language of shit and with how varied its usage has become, please read on.

A Glossary
of Shitty Language

bullshit	untrue
cool shit	that's great
deep shit	trouble
give a shit	care
holy shit	unbelievable
horseshit	untrue
no shit	are you certain?
oh shit!	oh no!
shit bird	unreliable person
shit box	junky car
shit faced	being drunk
shit for brains	stupid
shit happens	bad things happen
shit head	dumb person
shit hole	undesirable location
shit house	bathroom
shit kicker	rural person

shit list	**subject of anger**
shit probe	**colonoscopy**
shit storm	**bad results**
shitless	**frightened**
shitty deal	**bad bargain**
stepped in shit	**made a bad move**
sure as shit	**certain**
talking shit	**lying**
crock of shit	**no truth to it**
tough shit	**too bad**
hot shit	**person with a big ego**
shit hit the fan	**everything went wrong**
shit or get off the pot	**make a decision**
get your shit together	**improve**

Comedian George Carlin, on Shit

"You can be shit faced, shit out of luck, or have shit for brains. With a little effort you can get your shit together, find a place for your shit, or decide to shit or get off the pot. You can smoke shit, buy shit, sell shit, lose shit, find shit, forget shit, and tell others to eat shit. Some people know their shit while others can't tell the difference between shit and shineola. There are lucky shits, dumb shits, crazy shits, and sweet shits. There is bull shit, horse shit, and chicken shit. You can throw shit, sling shit, catch shit, and duck when the shit hits the fan. You can give a shit or serve shit on a shingle. You can find yourself in deep shit or be happier than a pig in shit. Some days are colder than shit and some days are hotter than shit. There are times you feel like shit. You can have too much shit or not enough shit. Some music sounds like shit, and sometimes you feel like shit. Sometimes everything you touch turns to shit."

ABOUT THE AUTHOR

Jerry Jampolsky, M.D., is a graduate of Stanford Medical School and a former faculty member of the University of California School of Medicine in San Francisco, where he has held fellowships in child psychiatry at Langley Porter Neuropsychiatric Institute. He is an internationally recognized authority in the fields of psychiatry, health, and education.

In 1975 Jerry established the original International Center for Attitudinal Healing in Tiburon, California which later moved to Sausalito, California. The Center has free support groups for children and adults who are facing catastrophic illnesses, loss and grief, school programs called "The Power to Choose," as well as multidisciplinary programs for schools and families. A very popular program is "Person to Person" which consists of support groups for people who want to learn how to incorporate Attitudinal Healing Principles into their own lives. There are programs called "Aging with Attitude," and recently support programs for people suffering from financial loss and fear were added.

Through the last 30 years, Jerry and and his wife, Diane Cirincione, Ph.D., have lectured and consulted throughout the United States and in 54 foreign countries, giving presentations covering psychology, psychiatry, mental and physical health, the power of change, attitudinal healing, grief and death and other life transitions, interpersonal relationships, and education and business as they affect both our personal and professional lives. Their work is often referred to as practical spirituality.

In 1987 Jerry and Diane founded the Aids Hot Line and helped create a poster that is used by the World Health Organization which pictures a little boy saying, "I have Aids. Please hug me. I can't make you sick." Today, there are independent Attitudinal Healing Centers and Groups throughout the world including North, Central, and South America; Western and Eastern Europe; the Near, Middle, and Far East; Africa, Australia, and New Zealand.

While working with and learning from people worldwide, Jerry has been the recipient of numerous awards, including the 2005 American Medical

Association's Excellence in Medicine Award: Pride in the Profession.

Books authored and co-authored with Diane Cirincione, Ph.D.:

Love is Letting Go of Fear
A Mini Course for Life
Finding Our Way Home
Forgiveness: The Greatest Healer of All
Change Your Mind, Change Your Life
Love is the Answer
Simple Thoughts That Can Change Your Life
Teach Only Love
Wake-Up Calls
Good-bye to Guilt
Out of Darkness into the Light
Shortcuts to God
Me First and the Gimme Gimmes

Jerry has also co-authored a book with his son, Lee Jampolsky, PhD, titled "Father and Son Relationships."

To learn more about Attitudinal Healing and Dr. Jerry Jampolsky go to:

www.JerryJampolsky.com
www.AttitudinalHealingInternational.org
www.ArchitectsOfANewDawn.com
www.AOAND.com

"The Oh Shit Factor" is available at:

www.ohshitfactor.com
www.Amazon.com

It is also available on Amazon as an eBook and on Kindle.

To contact Dr. Jampolsky to give a lecture or workshop, inquire at:

info@ohshitfactor.com

Made in the USA
Las Vegas, NV
06 March 2022

45155848R00066